As the Roses Pile

Poetry Collection

Pamela Colón

As the Roses Pile

As the Roses Pile

For **Ms. Hemming** and **Mr. Davis**, who
taught me how to give my words a voice.

And for my friends and family, who have
always allowed me to express myself.

IV

Smells like a dead rose,
that has been waiting on attention.

The delicacy has been washed away by the
horror of human hands
and the greediness of the world.

It is a rose that has forgotten water and
admiration; and time has turned its sweet petals
into ashes, a shattered personality existing
undiscovered, hidden away for a long time and
never found, the sweetness somewhere darker
than the bottom of a well.

As the flower faded...
So did the little girl inside.

-Pamela Colón

TABLE OF CONTENTS

The Fracture

The Place Inside Me

The Fracture

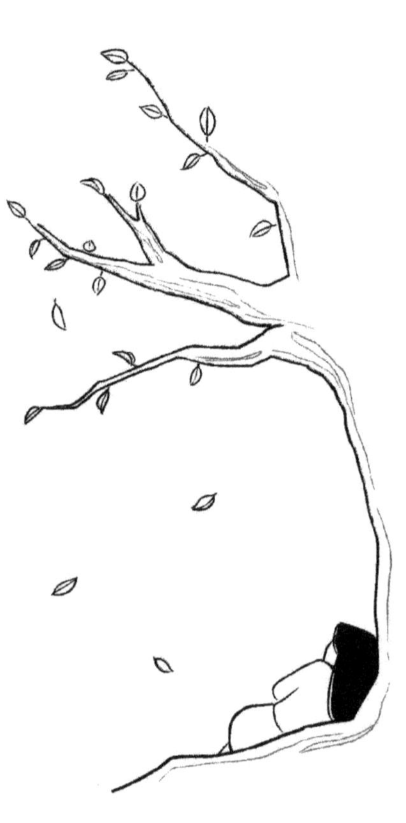

Prelude

Oh, little butterfly,
don't you cry.

Just because they
ripped your wings doesn't
mean you can't fly.

As the Roses Pile

My Reflection

Gazing out the window, I found her,
drenched in liquid sunshine.

Her piercing honey eyes mourned,
her tears unexposed,
So, she stayed there.

She **didn't** want anyone to know,
though I knew.

I remembered,
I'm lonely,
in the world
I'm lonely,
at home
I'm lonely,
in my heart.

I cried as I was drenched in liquid sunshine.

My tears disappeared with the
world's furor, as I watched her
from the street, through her window, she looked back at
me.

Solus at last.

As the Roses Pile

A Lost Soul

Her beautiful smile began to fade;
her mind became so crazed.

Her silhouette unraveled like loose thread,
she felt so unloved…
unwanted.

She was disappearing...

She heard whispers from the wilted,
the sound of sweet venom.

They said it would be okay once she crossed over,
but they had thorns.

Did she trust them?

"You will effloresce again just like spring,"
they persuaded her.

As she stepped into the garden…

she disintegrated,
and I have been lost since.

As the Roses Pile

Sad Sundays

You lather yourself in ideas, the
ones that make your mind run like
the fastest cheetahs in the wild.

Every Sunday is so bright…

until it rains, and
your ideas lose their shape.

Those are sad Sundays.

As the Roses Pile

Velvet

You took a piece of me when
you broke me.

I realized I am not whole, though
I once was before you.

After you… something else, I look
like a bear searching for food
before hibernation.

Perhaps like a rose that has
yet to bloom.

Though I do not find anything, I
keep looking.

There's no food…

As the Roses Pile

no water.

Desperate for nutrients,
desperate to feel whole.

I do not want the void,
or to search to fill it.

After piecing most of myself back together,
I realized something isn't right.

Something's gone
from my body,
mind, or my soul.

What could it have been?

I fix myself the best I can anyway,
trying to replace the missing piece.

The only thing I can seem to replace it with now
is my hate for you.

Then I discovered what you took from me

my trust,
my love,
my truths to you.

As the Roses Pile

Most of all,
you tore down the wall I built
that kept me whole like I
once was before you.

One Day

With her head held high,
she said,

"I will be free; all my worries
will soon be about me."

Then broke off another
piece of herself…
and gave it to a scrounger.

As the Roses Pile

Do you?

Do you want to be a piece, or
do you want to be a whole?

If you want to be whole,
don't let anyone break you.

Like the ocean waves,
merging into each other.

If you want to be a piece,
then let them take from you.

Let them slice into you and feed everyone,
they will have their cake and eat it too.

But you will no longer be you.

Do you want to be a piece,
or do you want to be a whole?

As the Roses Pile

I am the Empress

私は皇后です

I crowned myself with this title, to
silence all my doubts, my pain,
my insecurities.

Yet,

I still tremble.

As the Roses Pile

Open

He asked to see my rose,
but I only had my thorns to show.

I had already wilted, there
was nothing else to see.

Everyone has already taken
so many shards from me.

As the Roses Pile

Desires

Slowly,

at each whip he lashed with his words,
he took my desires from me…

my wants,
my needs,
the future I once foretold.

The desire to bear,
to be in holy matrimony.

Each desire, whip by
whip, carved away, from my serenity
by that poisonous tongue he owned.

As the Roses Pile

She isn't

She's not the same anymore.

Her kisses don't feel the same.

I can taste a new passion in them,
the passion of hatred.

Before, there was only pain.

She isn't

As the Roses Pile

Act I: The Plunge

Oh, little butterfly,
Don't you cry.
Just because they ripped your wings,
Doesn't mean you can't fly.

Even torn,
you remember the shape of air.
Even wounded, you carry
a flight no one can dare.

Oh, little butterfly,
Don't you cry.
They ripped your wings
because they can't be up as high.

Jealousy is…
a self-inflicted poison,
that will never reach the sky.

Oh, rest now, little butterfly…
Even broken wings grow back,
the ground was never the place
you called home.

As the Roses Pile

The Place Inside Me

As the Roses Pile

Depression House

This house holds the memory
of the monster I killed that day.
He was mean, he was angry,
ugly and stubborn.
He didn't sleep under my bed;
he hovered over me.

He intruded on my good dreams,
made them nightmares.
He made me sit in the corner
and danced in my thoughts.
This house holds the memory
of the monster I killed that day.

He showed me where to cut
and called it mercy.
He never lets me sleep;
he makes me play with my past.
This house holds the memory
of the monster I killed that day.

As the Roses Pile

He told me my friends
would be happy if I was dead.
He whispers
that I was a disgrace.
He said it would be better
if I jumped off the ledge.
This house holds the memory
of the monster I killed that day.

I told him,
"Hold my hand."
On the count of three,
together we will go.
I stepped back;
he jumped.

This house holds the memory
of the monster I tried to kill that day.
I relapsed…
he was back.

This house…
it has a monster
that comes to haunt me.
I will never be alive,
but I will never be alone.

Poison

It came knocking at my door,
the poison.
It entered through the vents.
I held my breath.
It appeared right before me.

I closed my eyes.
The tympanic membrane listens:
"Receive me, I will satisfy."
I don't want to give in
the poison.

It pushed me back; I still resist.
It traced my faults.
I screamed,
ecstatic.

The feeling,
like lying on a bed
of soft, wilted roses.
I let it all in,
the poison.

As the Roses Pile

Ashamed I feel.
The lust I have,
the poison.

It left my body,
drained me.
No longer feeling the high,
I'm left alone…
again.

Mirror

I'm going to set this place on fire, let
the ashes take the blame.
I wish you could be my passion, but
you left me with distaste.

I'm going to set your heart on fire,
leave your feelings out to tame. I wish
you could be my water, but I just want
to be the flame.

I'm going to set your soul on fire, let
the devil take your place.
You were supposed to be my desire, but
you left me full of ache.

As the Roses Pile

34

The Rain

I saw the rain fall, yet as I walked,
I didn't feel it touch me.

I kept trying to convince myself

I was human,
I wasn't dead…
but I was numb.

As the Roses Pile

36

The Light

The light was dimming,
no longer being fed by ambition.
The host,
no knowledge of the fade,
was sent to please
another agile being.

As the flames ignited in the foe,
fueled by the gasoline of the warrior,
not knowing why
they were already dead on the inside,
kept pushing through.

But the light was dead,
and a little spark fought for what's left.

The host woke up
after the spark's final cry.

As the Roses Pile

Poured water on the foe
to bring back their light.

38

The foe now drowns in sadness…
but at what cost, their life or mine?

Home

I don't know where home is.
You know,
that place that keeps you safe
within its enclosure?

That place where your mind
will never have to worry
about being trapped.
That place you go to
after you've had a rough day.

Home is where you make it,
but I've yet to make my nest.
Instead,
I've been intruding on everyone else's,
placing myself between their eggs.

I don't know where home is.

As the Roses Pile

Ashamed, I am.
My soul is homeless.
I am homeless.

You

Do you stop those demons from
calling your name? Do you tell
them to shut it and suck away
your pain?

They come when you're lonely,
they come when you're sad.
They are the ones
that put suicidal thoughts on
your mind.

You follow the path
of rose petals that wilted, but
when you get close,
you realize they were thorns.

They hurt your soul,
and you no longer want to fight.

As the Roses Pile

How can you stop yourself when
you're the demon that hides in
your head?

How can I stop myself from
screaming my name, when all I
want is to be in pain?
Because nothing else feels right,
because everything else is numb.

How can I stop myself from
withering away?

The Stitch

It's too much, isn't it?
And it hurts more, doesn't it?

It's excruciating, isn't it?
It seems so daft, doesn't it?

But you love the pain, don't you?

It isn't sufficient, though.
It isn't enough to fix…
me.

As the Roses Pile

Idle

My monster is idle.
But when my heart breaks, he
cries out to me.

I receive him.
He's the only constant.

Yet I always abandon him
when I'm content.

He doesn't judge me for it.
He just waits to pounce again.

As the Roses Pile

Serotonin

To put my demons to sleep,
I'd have to appease them.
Make friends with them,
feed them a sweet façade
just long enough
to plan my escape.

But the cycle is always the same:
they catch me,
drag me back,
wrap their hands around my mind
like they never left.

Their grip pulls me under,
a trance I don't notice
until I wake again
and realize where I am,
still here,
still breathing in their shadow.

As the Roses Pile

My demons tuck me in
again, patient and practiced.
And now I've become
the serotonin
they've grown immune to.

Best Friend

I don't drown my demons,
I give them a lifeline.

I don't shut them out,
the door's wide open.

Because they saved me.
They know me better,
keep me insane.

If I were like anyone else,
I would be disciplined.

I know that I'm durable,
so, I face them.

Keep your enemies close,
and your best friends closer.

As the Roses Pile

50

I Was Once Told

My depression once told me
I'll never be enough.

But the Empress in me said:
"We don't strive for enough;
we strive for more than."

As the Roses Pile

The Quiet Contract

The man I live with is never alone,
he has his roommates too.

In the next room over,
I hear the whispers.
The kind that crawl
instead of knock.

They argue with the quiet
and stain the air.
Sometimes they cry,
and it sounds like static.
Sometimes they just breathe,
and it sounds like thunder.

When I leave my room,
there is no sound.

As the Roses Pile

I'm untethered,
the outside soft and temporary,
waiting at the front door.

But then he's back,
and the hallway folds back in,
forgetting its light
before I can escape.

The man I live with is scarier than most,
teaching you how to smile at the world
while holding you hostage by the throat.

He keeps insisting
the lease has come to an end…
but I keep renewing.
Living is the only contract
I refuse to break.

And then the new day comes,
everything looks normal again.
Sunlight covers the bruises, the
ones unseen.

The man I live with walks past me,
then I remember how to inhale again.

The Mental Note

Keep to myself, that's all I do.
There is no one here to talk to.
Just these walls.

No one can understand the stress of my mind.
I tried to release it, but for some reason,
no one wants me to let go.
They want me to keep shut,
it's like holding back a bull.

Behind the chute,
you agitate him.
There's nothing he can do,
his anger boiling out of control
until he is finally set free.

As the Roses Pile

He sees red.
The roses?

The wrong move
can get you killed.

And throwing the muleta
doesn't help.

The anger and pain build up,
and he's about to explode.
He keeps trying to stop the problem,
but the problem carries on,
keeps running, making the
bull go in circles.

He thinks:
"I can't escape."

I must kill the problem
before the problem kills me.

On high alert he stays,
screaming out all of his pain,
but everyone just cheers,
entertained by someone else's pain.

He might win.
He might lose.

So, when my mind is released,
I will unleash an unknown wrath,
so toxic you will have
no choice but to listen.

As the Roses Pile

The Death of Life

There's a switch inside my intellectual self,
a switch that was once ignited.

But then my sight caught a glimpse
of a silver-tongued demon.
He offered me his hand.
Caught in his cologne of deceit,
it smelled so lavishing…
why not trust him?

He spun me around for years,
year after year, waltzing.
I was drowning in love.

But this year was different.
He spun me like he always did,
but never caught me like he always did.
He let me fall.

As the Roses Pile

Falling back into a dark place,
a cold place, a pale place.

I am now stuck, grounded.
My wishes now hollow,
my soul not knowing
what I wanted in life.
My senses becoming anesthetized.

Empty…
did I have a life?

All those years,
I had been spinning
in a web of fabrication,
wrapped in perjury.

He got to my switch,
that's what the demon did.
He turned it off.

No longer able to fight,
he sealed one more kiss,
and left a rose on my chest.

My eyes became dark,
and my skin as cold as ice.

Chaos

Open palms, taking a grip,
like holding onto an expensive, fragile thing,
a heart.

It's alive, beating in your own hand,
like a thud, thud, thud.

Oh, the end?

Soothing silhouettes won't calm you now.
You're out raging like a cow.

The mystery
of your screams seems to scar him,
but he sees that you're lying.

He waited for you all this time
and never noticed you were out dining.

As the Roses Pile

He waited till you sat,
pulled out a gun…
and the lights went out.

No one knows why he did it,
but you should know you were the one
who hid it.

He knew about your secret lover,
the one that sent you roses undercover.

He was crazy with a chaos,
no one knew he had that enigma.

He **didn't** want only lust,
he wanted to be loved,
like those little kids
who get unconditional love
from their mother.

But now he thought it was too late.

Right after he pulled the trigger to your head,
he **didn't** kill your lover, no…
he killed himself instead.

The Garden

99 black roses and one red,
99 bullets, and just one shot to the head.

Don't find yourself in a daze!
Pull the trigger and end our days.

20 seconds to run and hide, only 5 till they
catch you alive.

As the Roses Pile

Act II: Watching

A flight you can't take,
a burden that aches.
I love you in the sun,
but today I love you in the rain.

And when the wind blows,
I don't ask the sky for answers.
We know who took your wings,
the reckoning; theirs to keep.

Oh, little butterfly, smile.
Your soul is still here.
A borrowed sunrise,
the takeoff is near.

I keep the night from naming you,
I keep my fear inside.
When your wings remember light,
I'll step back and let you rise.

The Becoming

As the Roses Pile

Secret Doors

Yes… that will do.

That control you have over me,
I would do what makes you happy
and let myself break.
That seems like a better idea.

At least then
I wouldn't have to feel those
lashes from your tongue,
those that whip me into guilt.

Maybe I can learn to live without happiness.
Maybe I can be content
with its absence.

Though I have none with you,
you seem to find it with me.

So, I tuck away my box
of aspirations and dreams.

As the Roses Pile

My mind was clouded.
Then the storm came.

I realized that my soul was dehydrated,
and the only thing you had to serve
me with was venom.
I can't continue to drink that.
My soul is fading.

So, for my soul to feel alive,
I choose to walk away instead.

I will keep that door locked
and smile in your face
so, you can smile back at mine.

Because staying would destroy me,
and I refuse to become what breaks me.

My Heart

Because of my heart, life has been filled
with nothing but wailed cries.

Why am I such a good person?
Why do they take advantage of me?

They ravish my body and find my heart.
They extract it when they are ready and
fill it with thorns, my rosy heart.

Then they place it back and watch my
soul die.

As the Roses Pile

Parts of Me

All of him,
I chose all of him.
Yet he only ever reached
for parts of me.

The easy parts,
the bright parts,
the little sparks that feel like
your favorite song coming on,
or the first sweet bite of a savory treat.

He took those,
used them as if they were his to keep,
as if I was made of nothing
but the pieces that pleased him.

But the parts he touched
were the ones I cherished,
the ones I held close.
And somehow,
those are the ones
I'm missing now.

As the Roses Pile

Home?

I don't want to go home anymore.

Whispers of you are left behind,
intertwined within the walls.
Like unclaimed luggage,
I abandoned myself.

I roll around in this space,
so full of hollow emotions.

I was never enough to fight for.
You just loved the thought of me,
the spark I gave you when I ached,
like the first strike of a match
to a cigarette you crave after a long day.

In disbelief, I cried for your return.

When you left, I finally exhaled.

As the Roses Pile

But you returned in the fall to hold me close,
and now it's spring again,
and you have forsaken me.

Home…
I don't want to go home.

Butterfly

What I'll give to hear your voice
just once.

I'll listen as if it were the last time
I could indulge in music.

What I'll give to feel your warmth,
welcoming me like a tsunami.

What I'll give to see you smile at me.

What I'll give to just
forget you.

As the Roses Pile

Hurt for Me

Would you hurt for me?
Take all my pain
and destroy yourself for me?

Would you take my thoughts,
the ones that keep me up so late
as I fight my body
not to disintegrate?

Would you take my scars?
Not just the physical ones I've inflicted…
I want to keep those,
but the ones on my heart?

Would you take my anxiety?
You know, the thing that makes your breathing stop
for a moment,
when you think you'll die,
but instead, you live.

Would you take my hunger?
No, not that kind.

As the Roses Pile

The kind I must feed
is for love and understanding.

However, I never get it,
so now I'm starving.

Would you?

Would you take my thirst?
Except what I'm always parched for
is some poison
that would heal my carcass,
heal me
and make me whole again.

Though the naked eye can't see,
I can see.
And I need to be stitched to perfection
with some liquid potion.

Would you take my stress?
The thing that causes me to lose my hair,
my sleep,
and deteriorates my organs
one by one.
Yet it would take years
before I fall.

Here I am, hurting.
Would you hurt for me instead?

He Knows I Could

We savor the time we steal together like it
means something to us.
A tradition.

He knows me…
more than I have ever allowed myself to.
My demon…
or maybe I am his.

In his eyes, I am something untouched, soft
enough to be saved each time.
He doesn't want my soul.

But he doesn't hear the way my heart begs
to be desolated.

The sound of it splitting, aching,
calling out for something.
Knowing it will never be heard… never
understood.

As the Roses Pile

That's when I feel the most alone…
the most alive…

But he knows I would drown him if I could.
Slowly, with both hands,
while the air betrays him.

But I wouldn't… couldn't.
And even if I did,
it wouldn't matter.

He would rise again,
unafraid, forgiving.
He always survives with me.

He can breathe underwater after all.

So, I keep him,
and he keeps me… alone.

In that hollow space we share,
the untouched silence,

He knows I am most beautiful as I break.

I'm in Love

The thing is,
I love him.

I love the way he holds me
when I'm breaking,
crying, relapsing
in that cycle.

When he's not around,
I feel so happy but… forever numb.

After all these years with him,
I still don't understand it.

Why is it that
when I'm in the most pain,
I see everything more clearly?

Yet I always reach for the surface,
pull myself out.

Thank God I'm strong enough for that…

As the Roses Pile

Because if I wasn't,
I know where he would take me
if I let him keep me under.

I am not ready
for the promised land.

So, I'll stay here,
loving him
even if it's forever.

The Breakup

He always arrives on cue
to my chambers,
the ones he built
with chains for two.

He is the cause of it, for sure,
the cause of my mental breakdowns.

He brought a bunch of contrivances again.
The noose is his favorite,
but I can never bring myself to it.

I always shake my head,
but I'm tempted,
just like every other time
he has suggested.

He proposed we go to the bridge together this time.
Now this was new.

I really wanted to end things with him.
My curiosity peaked,
like that of a newborn

exploring their first instinct,
realizing what's needed
to stop the hunger pains.

He says he would like to end it there,
so he can then be with someone close to me,
a friend or a family member.
He says he doesn't mind at all.

No.

He was ready for his next
long-term relationship of misery.

I knew his plan.
He wants to live on.
He wants to leave me behind.

But my tears have stopped,
and now I think about the ones I love.

I told him
we should stay together a little longer.
I didn't want to share his demons
with my close ones.

So, to the bridge I won't go, no.

Not today.

Don't Take Me

Don't take me with you when you leave.
I want to stay here and watch my friends.

I am their shoulder to cry on,
their good listener,
their comedian,
their partner in crime.

I don't want to go when you leave.
You will cause my family pain.

I am the big sister, the little sister,
the daughter, the aunt,
the responsible one.

I want you to leave…
but I know you won't.

As the Roses Pile

You need my soul
because you have already latched onto it.

You used my pain,
my cries,
my abuse.

I will keep you a secret
until I decide
we can go together.

But don't take me with you today,
I don't want to be their despondent.

Door

A room full of ashes…
so beautiful
as a garden of wilted roses.

What remains… a life?

The ashes dance,
whispering memories,
a wish.

Someone was happy here,
but not for long.

Lust arrived,
left them numb…
craving more,
lost in their own hunger.

Disconnected.

What more can be asked for
when the pile has scattered
and the memories drift?

We are all now abandoned.

As the Roses Pile

As the Roses Pile

They cut out your thorns
so, you won't fight back.

When they sell your soul,
you can't have flaws.
Repudiation will follow.

They want you to be perfect and poised,
to bloom on time,
right under the moonlight.

Wilt when the hourglass
has passed its last grain of sand.

So just know,
they want to cut the thorns
to sell a soul.

You are not you.

As the Roses Pile

You are polished and groomed
for their amusement,
set to be sold.

Once you wilt,
no longer of use
to the oppressor who bought you,

Wasted like the rest of us
in a pile of desolate, beautiful roses.

Flower

Part ways with those
who do not water you.

Amend your petals
so, you won't wilt.

Strengthen your thorns,
build that wall,
don't look back.

No one is to be trusted
to pluck you.

As the Roses Pile

Passengers

Don't let passengers in.
They've already had enough to gawk at.

Stabbed in the back,
don't turn around
and let them find your chest.

You wouldn't survive,
grasping for oxygen while
choking on their lies.

There will be crocodile rain,
a side effect of their betrayal.

So don't let passengers in.

Don't let them be designated drivers.
Don't let them control where they take you,
especially when you know your way home.
It's best not to detour.

As the Roses Pile

They Will Tell It

They will tell it for you. The truth
they see fit,
the truth they've bestowed on you,
a truth that buries clues.

They will tell it…
but will you let them?
Let them fill the narrative? Or will
you fight back?

But if you fight back, they'll call it
defense, twist it into proof.

So, what do you do?

Me?

I'll let them fill it. Then I'll kill it.

As the Roses Pile

> I will not be blackmailed into being a
> ghost they want me to be,
> or recognizing a version of myself
> I never knew existed…

The Lady in Her Eyes

She was different.
She was taught to sit with her legs closed.
She was taught not to speak
unless she was spoken to.

She was different.
She was taught to take care of the home
and the children.
She was taught to cook the meals.

But she is different.

She learned to sit with
her legs up high.
She learned to interrupt
and speak her mind.

But she was different.
She didn't take care of the home
and let the children roam.

As the Roses Pile

She was different because
she cooked a meal
with the hearts of those
who taught her to be sane.

Morse Code

The puzzle in her eyes…

He wanted to solve it. He craved to
know more.
Where she's been,
what she has seen,
what she can tell him…
If only.

With her eyes,
the window to her soul, his soul would
scream back.

Hoping she would see him, hear him.

But she knew
he couldn't.
She knew
she couldn't.

The code was never to be understood.

As the Roses Pile

The puzzle was hers to keep, hers to hate,
hers to destroy.

We had hope,
but these pieces…
they were never meant to fit.

My Veins

Kiss me,
let me feel the pain
that will come after your betrayal
once you leave my lips.

Your love has numbed me.

The fire inside my eyes
burned me blind.

What could have been worse?

Inside my mind, I'm left with my empty thoughts,
alone again.

To be so full of life and emptiness.

Chasing temporary happiness
that will never fill me.

As the Roses Pile

Razor Sex

Not meant to be disclosed,
only meant to be endured in silence.

Ambushed, she was.
Now a grown woman,
she must learn self-control.

Because the razors moan her name,
calling her back once again.

She seals her ears,
but that won't do.

The urges seduce her through her consciousness,
teasing her, cornering her mind.

She aches for release, for
the pull of familiar pain, the
cycle she cannot name, the
mark it leaves behind.

As the Roses Pile

But it is not meant to be known what
she does to feel anything at all,
like nothing else can reach her.

To sustain
what nothing else can replace.

She hides the guilt for another day as
she looks in the mirror,
hearing echoes only she can
understand.

"To another night of indulgence."

Eye Smile

Smiles can hide so many things,
but the eyes could never.

You **can't** hear my pain,
and you will never see my pain.

Because your untrained eyes
will only want to see the happy things.

My eyes are tainted,
and have witnessed a soul die.

But no one will ever know.

They will never look close enough.

As the Roses Pile

In Time

I want to go back
to where the trees speak to me.

Once the breeze tells them a secret,
they all sing to me
to make me smile.
I have forgotten how…

Now I walk by the trees,
and they ignore me.

I have matured too much…
endured too much.

My mind no longer pure
to kiss the wind.

So, I'll lay here by the roots
until it's time to try again.

As the Roses Pile

Moon Goddess

A glimpse of her silhouette
hypnotized him.

He saw her,
couldn't move.

The moon goddess escaped from
the shadows to dance for him.

He froze in time
as he watched her facade, unable
to touch the goddess she was.

She leaned in and placed a kiss
that broke him free.

As the Roses Pile

But she no longer danced for him.

As he fell to his knees, he heard:
"Take care, my old friend."

Lovely Moon, Lonely Moon

Sometimes loneliness is love,
to look out the casement
and witness the full moon.

The moonlight wakes the earth
and moves the sea.
The moon shines over the black roses
and breaches their petals.

Just like when you bore into me
and churn me from my consciousness.

I am never fully ripe for you,
yet you take me anyway.

But loneliness…
loneliness loves me.

Lovely Moon, Lonely Moon

As the Roses Pile

Because I am lonely when you are gone,
and those are the best times for me.

The placid… peace.

Because I am alone,
and without your interruption,
then I am truly free.

I am in love with loneliness;
the loneliness you cast me.

Moon Flowers

Have you ever had a taste
for the moon flowers up in space?
Have you ever had a taste
for the things that **don't** go your way?

The kind that opens only once,
then fold themselves without a sound,
a soft goodbye you almost miss
until you notice what's not around.

Have you ever chased a light
that dimmed just when you drew in close?
Stood there with your hands half-raised,
holding **nothing**… keeping most?

Some losses **don't** announce themselves;
they slip beneath your every day.

As the Roses Pile

> But still you look for small bright things,
> even knowing they won't stay.

Golden Kisses

I want to kiss the sun, repay it for its
kindness, for the glow it gave me,
for the way it always
returns after a storm and
makes life bloom again.

I want to kiss the sun and repay it for
its kindness.

The nights I spent in shadow, the
moon comforted me.

But in the morning, the sun danced,
reminding me of a new day
where there are no mistakes yet, only
the chance to make new ones.

Though you **don't** stay as long
in the winter,
I forgive you every sunrise.

Ecclesiastes

I went searching for a sunrise, but
the morning vanished into fog.

The road fell away beneath me,
a white silence swallowing every mile,
yet something inside whispered: endure.

Sightless, I drifted closer to him,
drawn by a presence I could feel in the bones,
not in the light.

It was as if the unseen held my hand
while the visible world disappeared.

When the fog finally loosened its hold,
the lesson he left clung to my heart
like a fingerprint I can't wash off,
gentle, but impossible to forget.

As the Roses Pile

Now the sun rises differently
for me, not in the sky,
but deep in the quiet places.

A light that finds me only
when I close my eyes.

Another Road

I don't know what I'm doing here.

Each day I drift,
weightless and unfinished.

I laugh,
but nothing in it makes me feel alive.

I cry oceans of tears,
but they are translucent.

There is a path before me,
but I cannot take it.

I am fixed in place,
like a corroded statue.

And the closer I move toward it,
the farther it slips away.

As the Roses Pile

So, what am I meant to do?

Carve my own?

How cruel that sounds.
How heavy… how important.

But if I must,
if that is what is asked of me,
then I will.

Not for myself,
but for the ones who come after,
the ones who may need it most.

I will be strong enough.
I will endure it,
even if survival
feels like dying.

Act III: Goodbye Mother of Wings

Oh, little butterfly,
how do you feel?
Up in the sky,
your wings are strong as steel.

Now go, **and don't** worry.
Me? I'll be okay.
My wings never grew back,
I chose to guard the sky and stay.

The fallen, they need a guide…
those who lose their voice in flight,
in a void full of thieves.

Now go, little butterfly.

I have a new friend coming,
miles from me.

As the Roses Pile

They will be just like you,
and they will rise again too.

When one falls,
the other lights the path.

Go, little butterfly.
I'm the one that gets to stay.